D1717079

Shearers 16.95

RESOURCE CENTRE

POEMS NOT TO BE MISSED

an anthology
by
Susan Hill

illustrated by
Debby Strauss

A Keystone Picture Book
Produced by Martin International Pty Ltd
South Australia
Published in association with
Era Publications, 220 Grange Road, Flinders Park,
South Australia 5025

Iypeset by Iypecraft, Adelaide
Printed in Hong Kong
First published 1991

National Library of Australia
Cataloguing-in-Publication Data
Poems not to be missed.
Includes index
ISBN 0 947212 73 6.
ISBN 0 947212 72 8 (pbk.).

1. Children's poetry. I. Hill, Susan (Susan Elizabeth). II. Strauss, Debby, 1965-

808.810083

Available in:
the United Kingdom from
Ragged Bears, Andover, Hants
(hardcover)

Arncliffe Publishing.
Roseville Business Park, Leeds
(paperback)

Canada from
Vanwell Publishing Ltd
1 Northrup Crescent,
St Catharines, Ontario
(hardcover & paperback)

Acknowledgements

I'm just going out for a moment, from *Wouldn't you like to know* (1977), reprinted by permission of Michael Rosen and Andre Deutsch Ltd, London. **Macavity: the mystery cat,** from *Old Possum's Book of Practical Cats,* ©1939 by T.S.Eliot and renewed 1967 by Esme Valerie Eliot, reprinted by permission of Harcourt Brace Jovanovich, Inc. **Matilda,** from *Cautionary Tales for Children,* reprinted by permission of the Peters Fraser & Dunlop Group Ltd, London. **The Adventures of Isabel,** from *The Bad Parents' Garden of Verse* (1936) reprinted by pemission of Curtis Brown Ltd. copyright ©1936 by Ogden Nash, renewed ©1963 by Ogden Nash**. The Land of the Bumbley Boo**, from *Silly Verse for Kids* (1959)**,** reprinted by permission of Spike Milligan Productions Ltd, London. **Children Lost,** from *A Paddock of Poems* (1987) reprinted by permission of the author and John Johnson Ltd. **My Country,** reprinted by permission of Curtis Brown (Aus) Pty Ltd. **Dream of a Bird,** from *Rattling in the Wind,* reprinted by permission of the author.

Contents

Introduction 4

The Ordinary becomes Special:
I'm just going out for a moment 5
Macavity: the mystery cat 6
From a Railway Carriage 9

Play and Nonsense:
The Land of the Bumbley Boo 10
Song of the Witches 12
Matilda, Who Told Lies and Was Burned to Death .. 13
The Adventures of Isabel 16
There was an Old Man with a Beard 20
Twinkle, Twinkle Little Bat 20

From the Heart:
Question 21
Children Lost 22
My Country 26
Dream of a Bird 28
Index by title 30
Index by author 31
Index by first line 32

Introduction

The poems in this anthology were selected by children. They are poems they wanted to share and read again. The poems highlight some of the themes poets write about and some of the styles that poets use.

In THE ORDINARY BECOMES SPECIAL, poets make animals, people and everyday events seem special. In PLAY AND NONSENSE poets turn words and ideas on their head and the serious becomes ridiculous. In FROM THE HEART poets share their feelings about people, places and friends, old and new.

Poems expand our views of what it is to be human, to feel joy, pain and affection for people, places and events. They engage our emotions and our sense of wonder and fun.

We keep the magic of poetry alive when we relax and take time to reflect, so the rhythm, the rhyme, the patterns of language, words and ideas can play together.

Enjoy these poems by letting them creep and curl into your imagination — they are poems not to be missed!

Susan Hill

The Ordinary Becomes Special

I'M JUST GOING OUT FOR A MOMENT

I'm just going out for a moment.
Why?
To make a cup of tea.
Why?
Because I'm thirsty.
Why?
Because it's hot.
Why?
Because the sun's shining.
Why?
Because it's summer.
Why?
Because that's when it is.
Why?
Why don't you stop saying why?
Why?
Tea-time why.
High-time-you-stopped-saying-why-time.

What?

Michael Rosen

MACAVITY: THE MYSTERY CAT

Macavity's a Mystery Cat: he's called the Hidden Paw—
For he's the master criminal who can defy the Law.
He's the bafflement of Scotland Yard, the Flying Squad's
despair:
For when they reach the scene of crime — *Macavity's not
there!*

Macavity, Macavity, there's no one like Macavity,
He's broken every human law, he breaks the law of gravity.
His powers of levitation would make a fakir stare,
And when you reach the scene of crime — *Macavity's not
there!*
You may seek him in the basement, you may look up in
the air —
But I tell you once and once again, *Macavity's not there!*

Macavity's a ginger cat, he's very tall and thin;
You would know him if you saw him, for his eyes are
sunken in.
His brow is deeply lined with thought, his head is highly
domed;
His coat is dusty from neglect, his whiskers are un-
combed.
He sways his head from side to side, with movements
like a snake;
And when you think he's half asleep, he's always wide
awake.
Macavity, Macavity, there's no one like Macavity,
For he's a fiend in feline shape, a monster of depravity.
You may meet him in a by-street, you may see him in
the square —
But when a crime's discovered, then *Macavity's not
there!*

He's outwardly respectable. (They say he cheats at
cards.)
And his footprints are not found in any file of Scotland
Yard's
And when the larder's looted, or the jewel-case is rifled,
Or when the milk is missing, or another Peke's been
stifled,
Or the greenhouse glass is broken, and the trellis past
repair —
Ay, there's the wonder of the thing! *Macavity's not
there!*

And when the Foreign Office finds a Treaty's gone
astray,
Or the Admiralty lose some plans and drawings by the
way,
There may be a scrap of paper in the hall or on the
stair —
But it's useless to investigate — *Macavity's not there!*
And when the loss has been disclosed, the Secret
Service say:
'It *must* have been Macavity!' — but he's a mile away.
You'll be sure to find him resting, or a-licking of his
thumbs,
Or engaged in doing complicated long-division sums.

Macavity, Macavity, there's no one like Macavity,
There never was a Cat of such deceitfulness and
suavity.
He always has an alibi, and one or two to spare:
At whatever time the deed took place — MACAVITY
WASN'T THERE!
And they say that all the Cats whose wicked deeds are
widely known
(I might mention Mungojerrie, I might mention
Griddlebone)
Are nothing more than agents for the Cat who all the
time
Just controls their operations: the Napoleon of Crime!

T.S. Eliot

FROM A RAILWAY CARRIAGE

Faster than fairies, faster than witches,
Bridges and houses, hedges and ditches;
And charging along like troops in a battle,
All through the meadows the horses and cattle;
All of the sights of the hill and the plain
Fly as thick as driving rain:
And ever again, in the wink of an eye,
Painted stations whistle by.

Here is a child who clambers and scrambles,
All by himself and gathering brambles;
Here is a tramp who stands and gazes;
And there is the green for stringing the daisies!
Here is a cart run away in the road
Lumping along with man and load;
And here is a mill, and there is a river
Each a glimpse and gone for ever!

Robert Louis Stevenson

Play and Nonsense

THE LAND OF THE BUMBLEY BOO

In the Land of the Bumbley Boo
The people are red, white and blue,
They never blow noses,
Or ever wear closes,
What a sensible thing to do!

In the Land of the Bumbley Boo
You can buy Lemon pie at the Zoo;
They give away Foxes
In little Pink Boxes
And Bottles of Dandylion Stew.

In the Land of the Bumbley Boo
You never see a Gnu,
But thousands of cats
Wearing trousers and hats
Made of Pumpkins and Pelican Glue!

Chorus
Oh, the Bumbley Boo! the Bumbley Boo!
That's the place for me and you!
So hurry! Let's run!
The train leaves at one!
For the Land of the Bumbley Boo!
The wonderful Bumbley Boo-Boo-Boo!
The Wonderful Bumbley BOO ! ! !

Spike Milligan

SONG OF THE WITCHES

Double, double toil and trouble;
Fire burn and cauldron bubble.
Fillet of a fenny snake,
In the cauldron boil and bake;
Eye of newt and toe of frog,
Wool of bat and tongue of dog,

Adder's fork and blind-worm's sting,
Lizard's leg and howlet's wing,
For a charm of powerful trouble,
Like a hell-broth boil and bubble.

Double, double toil and trouble;
Fire burn and cauldron bubble.
Cool it with a baboon's blood,
Then the charm is firm and good.

Macbeth: IV.i. 10-19; 35-38
William Shakespeare

MATILDA, WHO TOLD LIES, AND WAS BURNED TO DEATH

Matilda told such Dreadful Lies,
It made one Gasp and Stretch one's Eyes;
Her Aunt, who, from her Earliest Youth,
Had kept a Strict Regard for Truth,
Attempted to Believe Matilda:
The effort very nearly killed her,
And would have done so, had not She
Discovered this Infirmity.

For once, towards the Close of Day,
Matilda, growing tired of play,
And finding she was left alone,
Went tiptoe to the Telephone
And summoned the Immediate Aid
Of London's Noble Fire-Brigade.

Within an hour the Gallant Band
Were pouring in on every hand,
From Putney, Hackney Downs and Bow,
With Courage high and Hearts a-glow
They galloped, roaring through the Town,

"Matilda's House is Burning Down!"
Inspired by British Cheers and Loud
Proceeding from the Frenzied Crowd,
They ran their ladders through a score
Of windows on the Ball Room Floor;
And took Peculiar Pains to Souse
The Pictures up and down the House,
Until Matilda's Aunt succeeded
In showing them they were not needed
And even then she had to pay
To get the Men to go away!

It happened that a few Weeks later
Her Aunt was off to the Theatre
To see that Interesting Play
The Second Mrs Tanqueray.
She had refused to take her Niece
To hear this Entertaining Piece:
A Deprivation Just and Wise
To Punish her for Telling Lies.

That Night a Fire *did* break out —
You should have heard Matilda Shout!
You should have heard her Scream and Bawl,
And throw the window up and call
To People passing in the Street —
(The rapidly increasing Heat
Encouraging her to obtain
Their confidence) — but all in vain!
For every time She shouted "Fire!"
They only answered "Little Liar!"
And therefore when her Aunt returned,

Matilda, and the House, were Burned.

Hilaire Belloc

THE ADVENTURES OF ISABEL

Isabel met an enormous bear,
Isabel, Isabel, didn't care:
The bear was hungry, the bear was ravenous,
The bear's big mouth was cruel and cavernous.
The bear said, Isabel, glad to meet you,
How do, Isabel, now I'll eat you!
Isabel, Isabel, didn't worry,
Isabel didn't scream or scurry,
She washed her hands and
  she straightened her hair up,
Then Isabel quietly ate the bear up.

Once in a night as black as pitch
Isabel met a wicked witch.
The witch's face was cross and wrinkled,
The witch's gums with teeth were sprinkled.
Ho ho, Isabel! the old witch crowed,
I'll turn you into an ugly toad!
Isabel, Isabel, didn't worry,
Isabel didn't scream or scurry,
She showed no rage, she showed no rancor,
But she turned the witch into milk and drank her.

Isabel met a hideous giant,
Isabel continued self-reliant.
The giant was hairy, the giant was horrid,
He had one eye in the middle of his forehead.
Good morning, Isabel, the giant said,
I'll grind your bones to make my bread.
Isabel, Isabel, didn't worry,
Isabel didn't scream or scurry.
She nibbled the zwieback that she always fed off,
And when it was gone, she cut the giant's head off.

Isabel met a troublesome doctor,
He punched and he poked till he really shocked her.
The doctor's talk was of coughs and chills
And the doctor's satchel bulged with pills.
The doctor said unto Isabel,
Swallow this, it will make you well.
Isabel, Isabel, didn't worry,
Isabel didn't scream or scurry.
She took those pills from the pill concoctor,
And Isabel calmly cured the doctor.

Isabel once was asleep in bed
When a horrible dream crawled into her head.
It was worse than a dinosaur, worse than a shark,
Worse than an octopus oozing in the dark.
Boo! said the dream, with a dreadful grin,
I'm going to scare you out of your skin!
Isabel, Isabel, didn't worry,
Isabel didn't scream or scurry,
Isabel had a cleverer scheme;
She just woke up and fooled that dream.
Whenever you meet a bugaboo
Remember what Isabel used to do.
Don't scream when the bugaboo says Boo!
Just look it in the eye and say, Boo to you!
That's how to banish a bugaboo;
Isabel did it and so can you!
Boooooo to you.

Ogden Nash

There was an Old Man with a beard,
Who said, "It is just as I feared! —
Two Owls and a Hen, four Larks and a Wren,
Have all built their nests in my beard!"

Edward Lear

Twinkle, twinkle, little bat,
How I wonder what you're at!
Up above the world you fly,
Like a tea tray in the sky.

Lewis Carroll

QUESTION

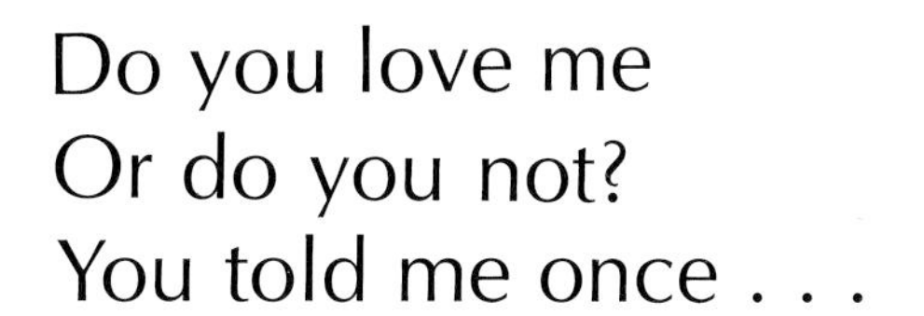

Do you love me
Or do you not?
You told me once . . .

. . . but I forgot.

Anonymous

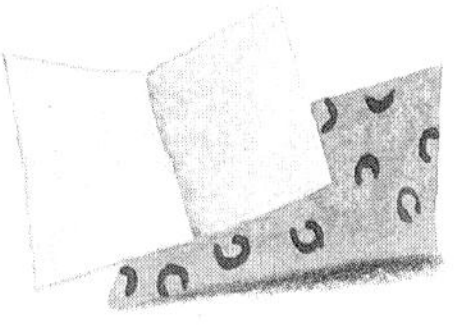

CHILDREN LOST

On a lonely beach the old wreck lies
With its rusted ribs and sides,
To the biting lash of the salty wind
And the drive of the flooding tides.

Years ago it was wrecked, they said,
Wrecked where the loud winds blew.
All hands were lost in the sad affair
And the women and children too.

It's there I went on a moonlit night
Where the cliffs slope wild and steep,
And suddenly came a shout and cry
As the ship awoke from sleep.

She had her masts and sails again,
No longer a broken wreck,
While the sailors sang as they hauled the ropes
And the children played on the deck.

They shouted and played on the heaving deck
Or sat at their cabin tea
While the sly winds filled the swelling sails
On the toss of the cunning sea.

But no one knew and no one dreamed . . .
Beware of the sailor's boast
That says he's master of the sea
Or king of the rugged coast.

For I heard it all on a moonlit night,
The eager waves' wild roar
And the cries of the crew as the great sea threw
That broken ship ashore.

Where, where the children? Never a sound
On the reef's cold rock and stone,
For the selfish sea had taken them all
And kept them for its own.

"Perhaps, perhaps . . .," the sea kings said
To the children deep and drowned,
"We will let you go to the shore again
but by this bond you're bound.

"That you are the children of the sea,
Of the waves and the dolphin's track
On a moonlit night we'll set you free
But then we'll call you back . . .

"On the ghostly beach you will play your games
But far from the cheerful town
Then back we'll call you, children, back
When the cold-eyed moon goes down."

Or so it seemed to come to me
In the voice of the wind and the tide,
As I stood on the beach where the moonlight fell
On the ship with the broken side.

And did I hear and could I hear
The sound of some voices there?
Did figures form and vanish again
In the strange and haunted air?

How shall I tell you what I felt
And how will you understand
What, by the moon, my own eyes saw —
Small footprints in the sand!

Max Fatchen

MY COUNTRY

The love of field and coppice,
Of green and shaded lanes,
Of ordered woods and gardens
Is running in your veins.
Strong love of grey-blue distance,
Brown streams and soft, dim skies —
I know, but cannot share it,
My love is otherwise.

I love a sunburnt county,
A land of sweeping plains,
Of ragged mountain ranges,
Of droughts and flooding rains.
I love her far horizons,
I love her jewel-sea,
Her beauty and her terror —
The wide brown land for me!

The stark white ring-barked forests,
All tragic to the moon,
The sapphire-misted mountains,
The hot gold hush of noon,
Green tangle of the brushes
Where lithe lianas coil,
And orchids deck the tree-tops,
And ferns the warm dark soil.

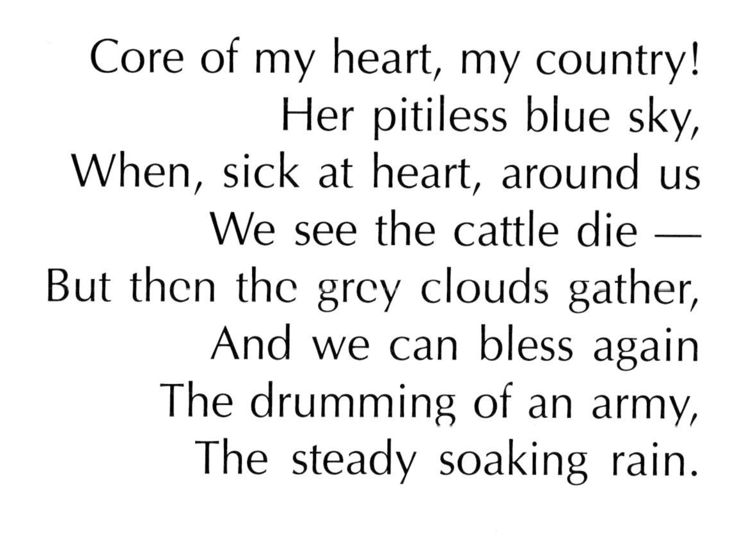

Core of my heart, my country!
Her pitiless blue sky,
When, sick at heart, around us
We see the cattle die —
But then the grey clouds gather,
And we can bless again
The drumming of an army,
The steady soaking rain.

Core of my heart, my country!
Land of the rainbow gold,
For flood and fire and famine
She pays us back threefold.
Over the thirsty paddocks,
Watch, after many days,
The filmy veil of greenness
That thickens as we gaze . . .

An opal-hearted country,
A wilful, lavish land —
All you who have not loved her,
You will not understand —
Though Earth holds many splendours,
Wherever I may die,
I know to what brown country
My homing thoughts will fly.

Dorothea Mackellar

DREAM OF A BIRD

You ask me, what did I dream?
I dreamt I became a bird.
You ask me, why did I want to become a bird?
I really wanted to have wings.
You ask me, why did I want wings?
These wings would help me fly back to my country.
You ask me, why did I want to go back there?
Because I wanted to find something I missed.
You ask me, what do I miss?
I miss the place where I lived as a child.
You ask me, what was that place like?
That place was happy, my family was close together.
You ask me, what I remember best?
I still remember, my father reading the newspaper.
You ask me, why I think of him?
I miss him and I'm sad.
You ask me, why I am sad?
I'm sad because all my friends have fathers.
You ask me, why does this matter?
Because my father is far away.
I want to fly to him like a bird.

Nga Bach Thi Tran

Index by title

Adventures of Isabel, The, ... 16
Children Lost 22
Dream of a Bird 28
From a Railway Carriage 9
I'm just going out for a moment 5
Land of the Bumbley Boo, The, ... 10
Macavity: the mystery cat 6
Matilda, Who Told Lies and Was Burned to Death .. 13
My Country 26
Question 21
Song of the Witches 12
There was an Old Man with a Beard.. 20
Twinkle, Twinkle Little Bat 20

Index by author

Anonymous; *Question* 21
Belloc, Hilaire; *Matilda, Who Told Lies and Was Burned to Death* 13
Carroll, Lewis; *Twinkle, Twinkle Little Bat* 20
Eliot, T.S.; *Macavity: the mystery cat* 6
Fatchen, Max; *Children Lost* 22
Lear, Edward; *There was an Old Man with a Beard* 20
Mackellar, Dorothea; *My Country* 26
Milligan, Spike; *The Land of the Bumbley Boo* 10
Nash, Ogden; *The Adventures of Isabel* 16
Rosen, Michael; *I'm just going out for a moment* ... 5
Shakespeare, William; *Song of the Witches* 12
Stevenson, Robert Louis; *From a Railway Carriage* 9
Tran Nga Thi Bach; *Dream of a Bird* 28

Index by first line

Do you love me 21
Double, double toil and trouble; 12
Faster than fairies, faster than witches, ... 9
I'm just going out for a moment 5
In the Land of the Bumbley Boo 10
Isabel met an enormous bear; 16
Macavity's a Mystery Cat: he's called the Hidden Paw 6
Matilda told such Dreadful Lies, ... 13
On a lonely beach the old wreck lies, ... 22
The love of field and coppice, ... 26
There was an Old Man with a beard, ... 20
Twinkle, twinkle, little bat, ... 20
You ask me, what did I dream? 28

RESOURCE CENTRE